The First Family of
HOPE

The OBAMAS

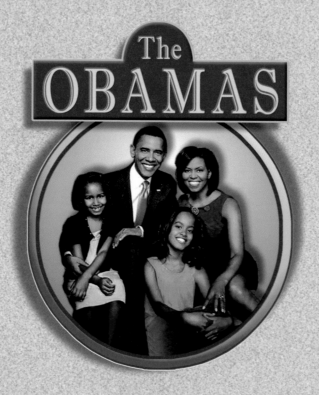

Barack

Michelle

Malia

Sasha

The Obama Family Tree

Obama Mania

Barack

Hal Marcovitz

Mason Crest Publishers

Produced by 21st Century Publishing and Communications, Inc.

MASON CREST PUBLISHERS INC.
370 Reed Road
Broomall, Pennsylvania 19008
(866) MCP-BOOK (toll free)
www.masoncrest.com

Printed in the United States of America.

First Printing

9 8 7 6 5 4 3 2 1

Library of Congress Cataloging-in-Publication Data

Marcovitz, Hal.
   Barack / Hal Marcovitz.
      p. cm. — (The Obamas : first family of hope)
   Includes bibliographical references and index.
   ISBN 978-1-4222-1477-0 (hardcover : alk. paper)
   ISBN 978-1-4222-1484-8 (pbk. : alk. paper)
   1. Obama, Barack—Juvenile literature. 2. Presidents—United States—Biography—Juvenile literature. 3. African American legislators—United States—Biography—Juvenile literature. 4. Legislators—United States—Biography—Juvenile literature. 5. United States. Congress. Senate—Biography—Juvenile literature. I. Title.
   E908.M369 2009
   973.32092—dc22
   [B]   2009001310

Publisher's notes:
All quotations in this book come from original sources, and contain the spelling and grammatical inconsistencies of the original text.

The Web sites mentioned in this book were active at the time of publication. The publisher is not responsible for Web sites that have changed their addresses or discontinued operation since the date of publication. The publisher will review and update the Web site addresses each time the book is reprinted.

Contents

Introduction

On November 7, 2008, just days after becoming the first African American elected president of the United States, Barack Obama was asked what books he was reading to prepare for the challenging job ahead. The president-elect cited only one author, telling reporters, "I have reread some of Lincoln's writings, which are always an extraordinary inspiration."

Throughout his years in the public eye, Mr. Obama has openly admired our nation's sixteenth president, Abraham Lincoln. As many people have noted, there are many superficial similarities between the two men. Lincoln overcame childhood poverty to become a successful lawyer in Illinois. He served several terms in the state legislature, but had limited experience in national government (a two-year term in the U.S. House of Representatives, 1847–48) before going to Washington, D.C., as the sixteenth president in 1861. Obama overcame childhood hardships to earn a law degree from Harvard, in the process becoming the first African American to serve as the president of the prestigious *Harvard Law Review*. Like Lincoln, Obama served several terms in the Illinois state legislature; in 2004, Obama was elected to one of Illinois's two seats in the U.S. Senate.

During his presidential campaign, Mr. Obama and his advisors often invoked the spirit of Abraham Lincoln. In February 2007, Obama chose Springfield, Illinois—the city where Lincoln had lived and worked—to declare his own candidacy for president. And on the historic election night, November 4, 2008—a night in which Obama won 53 percent of the popular vote and a landslide victory in the Electoral College—Obama used Lincoln's own

Barack Obama kept this portrait of Abraham Lincoln in his U.S. Senate office as an inspiration.

words in referring to the challenges that lie ahead for the United States. "While the Democratic Party has won a great victory tonight, we do so with a measure of humility and determination to heal the divides that have held back our progress," Obama told an enormous crowd gathered in Chicago's Grant Park. "As Lincoln said to a nation far more divided than ours, 'We are not enemies, but friends—though passion may have strained it must not break our bonds of affection.'"

The lines Obama quoted are from Lincoln's first inaugural address, delivered in March 1861. By that time, the greatest crisis of American history had already begun, as seven Southern states had decided to break away from the United States. Over the next four years, Lincoln faced grave and unprecedented challenges as he attempted to end the rebellion by the Southern states and preserve the Union as a whole.

Today, just as in 1861, the United States of America faces a critical moment in its history. As Obama prepared to take office, it became clear that the country had slipped into the worst economic recession since the Great Depression of the 1930s. Our military is engaged in conflicts in Iraq and Afghanistan, and we face potential threats from countries like Iran, North Korea, and Pakistan. A deadly terrorist attack on Mumbai, India, in December 2008 served as a reminder of the threat posed by radical Islamic groups. Other long-term challenges for the new president include addressing the issue of climate change, reforming our nation's health-care system, and shaping our nation to be competitive in the global economy of the twenty-first century. Some commentators have said that the new president faces greater and more diverse challenges than any previous president in American history.

Yet throughout the campaign Obama energized his followers with a message of hope—that if Americans work together, there is nothing they cannot accomplish. He told an audience in New Hampshire,

> ❝ Hope is not blind optimism. Hope is not sitting on the sidelines or shirking from a fight. Hope is that thing inside of us that insists, despite all the evidence to the contrary, that there is something greater inside of us. ❞

No one can solve America's problems on his or her own, and only time will tell whether President Barack Obama will successfully lead American citizens into the kind of historic change that this critical moment in our history requires. Obama's hope comes, in part, from the experiences of his own remarkable personal journey—a journey that has taken him from Hawaii and Indonesia to the White House. But it also comes, in part, from looking back to our past, and in particular, at the life and experiences of Abraham Lincoln. In a 2005 essay titled "What I See in Lincoln's Eyes," Obama wrote,

" In Lincoln's rise from poverty, his ultimate mastery of language and law, his capacity to overcome personal loss and remain determined in the face of repeated defeat—in all this, he reminded me not just of my own struggles. He also reminded me of a larger, fundamental element of American life—the enduring belief that we can constantly remake ourselves to fit our larger dreams. . . .

In his sheer energy, Lincoln captures a hunger in us to build and to innovate. It's a quality that can get us in trouble; we may be blind at times to the costs of progress. And yet, when I travel to other parts of the world, I remember that it is precisely such energy that sets us apart, a sense that there are no limits to the heights our nation might reach. **"**

OBAMA FAMILY TIMELINE

1600s to 1700s
Barack Obama's mother's ancestors immigrate to the American colonies from Europe.

1936
Barack Obama, Sr., Barack's father, is born in a small village in Kenya, Africa.

1964
Barack's parents, Barack Obama, Sr. and Ann Dunham are divorced.

1700s to 1800s
Michelle Robinson Obama's ancestors arrive in the American colonies as slaves.

1937
Michelle's mother, Marian Shields, is born.

1967–
Barack's mother marries Lolo Soetoro and moves the family to Soetoro's home country, Indonesia.

1850s
Michelle's great-great grandfather is born a slave in South Carolina.

1942
Barack's mother, Ann Dunham, is born in Kansas.

1971
Barack returns to Hawaii and lives with his grandparents.

1600   1900   1950   1982

1912
Michelle's grandfather, Fraser Robinson Jr., is born.

1959
Barack Obama, Sr. comes to America as a student.

1979
Barack graduates from high school and enrolls in Occidental College in Los Angeles, California.

1918
Barack's grandfather, Stanley Dunham, is born.

February 21, 1961
Barack Obama, Sr. and Ann Dunham are married.

1922
Barack's grandmother, Madelyn Payne, is born.

August 4, 1961
Barack is born in Honolulu, Hawaii.

1981
Barack transfers to Columbia University in New York City.

1935
Michelle's father, Fraser Robinson III, is born.

January 17, 1964
Michelle is born in Chicago, Illinois.

1982
Barack's father dies in Kenya, Africa.

1983

1988
Michelle graduates from Harvard Law School.

1988
Barack enters Harvard Law School.

1990
Barack is elected president of the *Harvard Law Review*.

1991
Barack graduates from Harvard Law School.

1995
Barack's first book, *Dreams from My Father*, is published.

1998
Barack and Michelle's first daughter, Malia, is born.

2001
Barack and Michelle's second daughter, Sasha, is born.

July 2004
Barack delivers keynote speech at Democratic National Convention.

November 2, 2008
Barack's grandmother dies in Hawaii.

November 4, 2008
Barack is elected the first African-American president of the United States.

January 20, 2009
Barack is sworn in as the 44th president of the United States.

1983 1995 2006 2009

1988
Barack visits his relatives in Kenya, Africa.

1985
Michelle graduates from Princeton University.

1985
Barack moves to Chicago, Illinois, to work as a community organizer.

1983
Barack graduates from Columbia University.

1996
Barack is elected to the Illinois State Senate.

1995
Barack's mother dies.

1992
Barack and Michelle are married.

1992
Barack begins teaching at the University of Chicago Law School.

August 2008
Barack is nominated as the Democratic candidate for the presidency.

February 10, 2007
Barack announces his candidacy for the office of president of the United States of America.

2006
Barack's second book, *The Audacity of Hope*, is published.

November 2004
Barack is elected to the U.S. Senate.

Barack Obama waves to the huge crowd in Grant Park, Chicago, on election night, 2008. After a long campaign, 240,000 supporters gathered to celebrate Obama's historic election as America's first African-American president, chanting, "This is our moment! This is our time!"

Playing Hard to Win

For Barack Obama, the long and grueling campaign for the presidency came to an end on a crisp November day in his hometown of Chicago, Illinois. After rising early to vote, Barack got in some last-minute campaigning, sat for interviews with reporters, and still managed to squeeze in two hours of hoops.

A PASSION AND A TRADITION

Basketball has been a passion for Barack since his childhood in Hawaii. Never good enough to even think about turning pro, Barack is still respected as a keen shooter who plays hard, hustles, and never lets bigger players intimidate him—which is exactly the way he plays politics.

Playing basketball on election day has been Barack's habit since he first entered politics. He finds the game helps him chill and forget about the pressures of running for political office. And so, on election day in 2008, as the world waited to see whether Barack would be elected the first African-American president in U.S. history, the candidate gathered some friends together for a vigorous game of basketball at a neighborhood gym. Said Alexi Giannoulias, one of Barack's friends who played hoops with the candidate,

> **❝ This is the most important day of his life, politically, and was such a huge day for this country. And to see him just as one of the guys, just playing ball, hanging out with friends, laughing. . . . On a personal level, it was just incredible to see. I'm so proud of him it's unbelievable. ❞**

Later that night, the day would end in a tremendous celebration in Chicago's Grant Park where Barack appeared before some 240,000 supporters and proclaimed, "This is our moment! This is our time!"

RISING EARLY TO VOTE

Barack's presidential campaign commenced on a bitterly cold day in the state capital of Springfield, where the Illinois senator announced his candidacy. Twenty-one months later, the last day of the campaign sped by like a whirlwind. Up before dawn, Barack and his wife, Michelle, got their children ready for school, then rushed off to Shoesmith Elementary School in the family's Hyde Park neighborhood to cast their ballots.

As soon as the Obamas entered, the crowd buzzed with excitement. For weeks, the polls had shown Barack leading his opponent, Senator John McCain of Arizona. Obama's commitment to change found favor among voters, who had grown weary of the Iraq War and were anxious for a new administration to ignite the country's

Barack Obama rebounds the ball during a basketball game with U.S. military personnel. Obama has always been passionate about basketball; he plays hard and never gives up, just as he did in his presidential campaign. He also finds that shooting hoops helps him chill and takes his mind off politics.

dismal economy and bring affordable health care to Americans. Said one Hyde Park voter, Amy Dru Stanley,

> **"This polling place is Barack's polling place, but it also epitomizes the essence of Hyde Park, where people have strong political beliefs and moral convictions across the political spectrum. This election represents the transformative possibility of U.S. constitutional democracy, and you're seeing it right here in this line of voters."**

ROLLING TO VICTORY

After voting, Barack headed to Indiana, one of the key battleground states. He attended a rally in Indianapolis, then returned to Chicago for dinner with his family.

That night, the Obamas gathered in front of a TV in a suite at the Hyatt Hotel in downtown Chicago to watch the returns come in. As soon as the networks started reporting the results, it was clear to everyone that Barack was on a roll. He started racking up state after state, building up a comfortable lead in **electoral votes** over McCain. When Pennsylvania and Ohio fell into Barack's column, his election seemed inevitable.

Then the network commentator made it official: Barack had crossed the magic threshold of 270 electoral votes. McCain was expected to concede at any moment. A few days later, a reporter asked Barack when it began to sink in that he would be sworn in as the nation's 44th president. He answered, "Well, I'm not sure it's sunk in yet."

CELEBRATION IN GRANT PARK

Once his victory was assured, Barack and the rest of his family were transported by **motorcade** to nearby Grant Park, where people gathered to hear his victory speech. Among the people waiting in the crowd were TV talk show host Oprah Winfrey, a dedicated Obama supporter, and the Reverend Jesse Jackson, a

(Left) President-elect Barack Obama appears with daughters Sasha and Malia and wife Michelle at the election night celebration in Grant Park, Chicago. (Right) The crowd in Grant Park cheers as Obama's election victory is announced. People all over the nation and the world celebrated his message of hope for the future.

longtime **civil rights** leader. Both are African Americans, and the enormity of what Barack had accomplished moved them deeply.

Winfrey, Jackson, and the others in the crowd anxiously awaited the words of the man who had achieved such an historic victory. A fiery and dynamic speaker, Barack did not disappoint them. Taking the stage before the sprawling crowd, he said,

> **❝ If there is anyone out there who still doubts that America is a place where all things are possible; who still wonders if the dream of our founders is alive in our time; who still questions the power of our democracy, tonight is your answer. ❞**

Barack Obama is held by his mother Stanley Ann Dunham in Honolulu, 1963. Barack was raised by Ann, a single mother, and he always missed his father's presence in his life. Growing up a child of a mixed-race marriage in multicultural Hawaii, Barack also struggled with his racial identity.

Discovering His Roots

His parents named him Barack, after the father he barely knew, but everyone called him Barry. He was born in Hawaii on August 4, 1961, to a black father and white mother during an era when mixed race marriages were still a rarity, and **miscegenation** was still a crime in some states.

Barack's mother was Stanley Ann Dunham, a white college student originally from Kansas. (Her father wanted a son; when his daughter was born, Stanley Dunham insisted on passing his name on to the girl.) Stanley Ann's husband, Barack Obama Sr., grew up in Kenya. The couple met when both were students at the University of Hawaii. Stanley Ann and Barack Sr. married in 1961 and divorced in 1964, mostly because Barack Sr. left Hawaii to study at Harvard University in Massachusetts, and had little to do with his young family. Later, Barack wrote about the emptiness he felt growing up without a father:

" My father was missing. He had left . . . and nothing that my mother or grandparents told me could obviate that simple, unassailable fact. Their stories didn't tell me why he had left. They couldn't describe what it might have been like had he stayed. "

America's Anti-Miscegenation Laws

In some states, laws banning mis-cegenation—marriage between the races—were still on the books as late as 1967, but that year the U.S. Supreme Court ruled a Virginia anti-miscegenation law was uncon-stitutional.

The case that led the court to strike down anti-miscegenation laws involved a couple, Richard and Mildred Loving, who married in 1958. Richard, who was white, and Mildred, who was black, lived in Caroline County, Virginia, where interracial marriage was illegal. To marry, the couple traveled 80 miles to Washington, D.C. After the ceremony, they returned to their home in Virginia, where they were eventually arrested.

The Lovings were each sentenced to a year in prison, but the judge agreed not to impose the sentence if the Lovings moved out of Virginia. The Lovings consented and moved to Washington. However, the Lovings challenged their convictions in court and, in 1967, the Supreme Court ruled that racial barriers cannot be used to prevent people from marrying.

In the years since the court found anti-miscegenation laws unconsti-tutional, millions of Americans of different races have married and given birth to children. In 2000, the U.S. Census Bureau reported that some 7 million Americans, or about 2.4 percent of the population, desig-nated themselves as multiracial.

Barack Obama's father, Barack Obama Sr., who was born in Africa. Barack was always curious about his father's African roots and later visited his native village in Kenya. A childhood without a father also made Barack want to be a hands-on dad with his daughters.

POVERTY IN INDONESIA

Barack hardly had a typical American childhood. At age 6, Barack's mother re-married, this time to an Indonesian man, Lolo Soetoro; the family moved to the Indonesian capital of Jakarta where Barack saw intense poverty for the first time in his life. Recalled Barack,

Barack Obama with his stepfather Lolo Soetoro, mother Ann, and half-sister Maya in Jakarta, Indonesia, 1968. Barack's grade-school teacher in Jakarta recalled his essay about wanting to be president. "He didn't say what country he wanted to be president of . . . but he wanted to make everybody happy."

❝Beggars . . . seemed to be everywhere, a gallery of ills—men, women, children, in tattered clothing matted with dirt, some without arms, others without feet, victims of scurvy or polio or leprosy walking on their hands or rolling down the crowded sidewalks in jerry-built cars, their legs twisted behind them like contortionists'.❞

While living in Indonesia, Stanley Ann gave birth to Barack's half-sister, Maya. By 1971, the marriage between Soetoro and Barack's mother was falling apart, so Stanley Ann sent Barack and Maya back to Hawaii to live with her parents.

BACK IN HAWAII

In Hawaii, Barack attended Punahou School where he made the varsity basketball team. Barack wasn't a starter, but he had a deadly jump shot and earned the nickname "Barry O'Bomber."

Barack's high school years were cool, but they were also marked by confusion. As a teenager, he had white, black, Asian, and native Hawaiian friends, but nobody else seemed to be of mixed race. At school, he would hang with his black friend Ray, then come home and chill with his white family. Barack recalled,

Barack and his grandparents, Madelyn and Stanley Dunham, in Hawaii, 1979. The Dunhams raised and mentored Barack as a teen. According to a friend, "In the absence of [Barack's] father, there was not a kinder, more understanding man than Stanley Dunham." Sadly, neither grandparent lived to see Barack elected president.

> **"** Sometimes, I would find myself talking to Ray about *white folks* this or *white folks* that, and I would suddenly remember my mother's smile, and the words I spoke would seem awkward and false. **"**

To cope with his confusion over his racial identity, Barack experimented with alcohol and drugs. Eventually, Barack learned to accept his unique racial status. After graduating from Punahou, he enrolled in Occidental College in California, then transferred to Columbia University in New York City.

VISITING KOGELO

Barack graduated from college in 1982, first taking a job as a writer for a financial services corporation in New York City. The job paid well, but Barack did not feel fulfilled. He wanted to help people improve their lives, so he found a job in Chicago as a community organizer, working on public housing issues, school reform, and hazardous waste cleanup. He spent five

Barack Means "Blessed"

Barack Obama's first name is derived from a word that means "blessed by God" in Hebrew, Arabic, and Swahili.

Barack's middle name is Hussein, a common name in the Islamic community. A Christian, Barack was given his middle name by his parents to honor his grandfather, a Kenyan Muslim named Hussein. Many Muslims name their children Hussein to honor Hussein ibn Ali, the grandson of the prophet Muhammad who gave his life in defense of Islam.

During the 2008 presidential election, Barack's middle name became something of a campaign issue as many political opponents used it to incite hatred by making vague connections between Barack and Saddam Hussein, the Iraqi dictator overthrown by an American-led invasion in 2003. Defenders were quick to point out that Hussein was also the name of Jordan's late King Hussein, one of America's staunchest allies in the **Middle East**.

years as a community organizer, then entered Harvard Law School in 1988.

Before beginning his law studies, Barack traveled to Kenya and the village of Kogelo, his father's hometown. Barack had barely known his father—when Barack was 11, his father had returned to Hawaii to hang with Barack, but the brief visit was awkward and tense and the two failed to forge an emotional bond. It was the last time Barack saw his father. Barack Sr. died in an automobile accident in 1982.

In Kenya, Barack met his half-siblings, cousins, nieces, and nephews as well as his father's stepmother, Sarah Hussein Onyango, who had raised Barack Sr. since childhood. Barack

Barack poses with his Kenyan relatives, Africa, 1988. Making a connection with them was important to Barack; he realized how hard it had been for Barack Sr. to get to college in America. Barack's step-grandmother, Sarah Onyango Obama, whom he calls "Granny," is in the gold dress in front.

learned about his father from the woman, whom he called "Granny," gaining a new insight into the struggles his father had to overcome to lift himself out of the poverty of an African village to attend college in America. Granny recalled how Barack Sr. studied for months to win a **scholarship** to study at the University of Hawaii. She said,

> **Every night, and during his lunch hours, he would study his books and do the lessons in his notebooks. A few months later, he sat for the exam. . . . The exam took several months to score, and during this wait he was so nervous he could barely eat. He became so thin that we thought he would die. One day, the letter came. I was not there to see him open it. I know that when he told me the news, he was still shouting out with happiness.**

Law Review President

After a year at Harvard, Barack found a summer job at a Chicago law firm, where he was mentored by a young African-American attorney, Michelle Robinson. A romance soon developed. Returning to Harvard, Barack was elected president of the *Harvard Law Review* by his fellow students. The *Law Review* is the college's prestigious publication that provides commentary on important legal cases; during its more than a century of existence, an African American had never been elected president. The competition among the *Law Review's* 70 staff members was fierce—election as editor virtually guarantees landing a job at a big-time law firm after graduation—but in the end the election came down to a contest between Barack and Kenneth Mack, another African-American student.

After Barack won the election, Mack congratulated his rival by embracing him. Mack's gesture showed Barack that even though he lost the election, he could still celebrate the history-making occasion. Said Barack,

Barack Obama as the first African-American president of the *Harvard Law Review*. Barack acknowledged others before him who had worked to end racial barriers, saying that "for every one of me there are a hundred, or thousand, black and minority students who are . . . just as talented and never got the opportunity."

❝He held onto me for a long time. It was an important moment for me, because with that embrace I realized my election was not about me, but it was about us, about what we could do and what we could accomplish.❞

Barack during a 1990s voter registration campaign. In 1991 Barack's registration drive signed up tens of thousands of black voters in Chicago. As a result, Democrat Carol Moseley Braun was elected in 1992, the first black woman to serve in the U.S. Senate.

3

Connecting
with
the Voters

Among the people who read the stories about Barack's election to the presidency of the *Harvard Law Review* were editors at a New York publishing company. Enthralled by Barack's personal story of overcoming poverty in Indonesia, a broken family in Hawaii, and racial barriers at Harvard, they offered him a contract to write a book about his experiences.

DREAMS FROM MY FATHER

Published in 1995, *Dreams from My Father* traces Barack's personal journey and tries to define his place in society, making the case that if a young biracial man from Hawaii can accept the fact that he is a part of two races, Americans may be willing to accept a multiracial society as well.

Barack wrote the book after finishing law school. Meanwhile, he returned to Chicago where he headed a voter registration drive, and then worked for a Chicago law firm, specializing in civil rights cases. His political ambitions were still in the future, but there is no question that in *Dreams from My Father*, Barack issued a blueprint for his political philosophy. He wrote,

> **❝ I hear the spirit of . . . Jefferson and Lincoln. . . . I hear the voices of Japanese families interned behind barbed wire; young Russian Jews cutting patterns in Lower East Side sweatshops; dust-bowl farmers loading up their trucks with the remains of shattered lives.**
>
> **I hear . . . the voices of those who stand outside this country's borders, the weary, hungry bands crossing the Rio Grande. I hear all of these voices clamoring for recognition, all of them asking the very same questions that have come to shape my life, the same questions that I sometimes, late at night, find myself asking. . . . What is our community, and how might that community be reconciled with our freedom? How far do our obligations reach? ❞**

CHICAGO'S SOUTH SIDE

Barack and Michelle were married in 1992. Soon, two daughters, Malia and Sasha, joined the family. The couple bought a home in the Hyde Park section of Chicago's South Side and settled into a comfortable life.

In 1996, the seat representing the South Side of Chicago opened up in the state Senate. Barack's work in the voter registration drive had raised his profile among Democratic leaders. When Alice Palmer, the state senator for the South Side, chose not to seek re-election, Barack found support among Illinois Democratic leaders. He entered the race and easily won the post.

Barack Obama holds Malia, while his wife Michelle holds Sasha in 2002. After tension arose between Michelle and Barack over his spending so much time in the Illinois capital, he changed his priorities to spend more time with his wife and daughters.

POLITICS AND FAMILY

Barack's future seemed bright, but there were times of tension in the family. Michelle, a busy attorney and later a hospital administrator, found herself raising their two young daughters on her own as Barack spent much of his time in the state capital of Springfield, some 150 miles from the family's Chicago home. He also held down a job as a law school professor, lecturing to University of Chicago students at night. Said Barack,

Barack Obama teaches at the University of Chicago Law School. Barack enjoyed teaching constitutional law, saying, "All the tough questions land in your lap . . . and you need to be able to argue both sides. . . . I think that's good for one's politics. Teaching keeps you sharp."

❝ There are times when I want to do everything and be everything. I want to have time to read and swim with the kids and not disappoint my voters and do a really careful job on each and every thing that I do. And that can sometimes get me into trouble. ❞

Finally, Barack agreed to his wife's demands to pay more attention to his family, a decision that ultimately caused a political backlash. In 1999, he took his family to Hawaii for a vacation at a time when a crucial bill on gun control legislation came to the Senate floor for a vote. When Malia, then 18 months old, became ill, Barack refused to cut his vacation short to return to Springfield for the vote.

Michelle Obama

Born on the South Side of Chicago, Michelle Obama won an academic scholarship to Princeton University and then a law degree from Harvard. After practicing law in Chicago, she took a job as an aide to Mayor Richard M. Daley, then headed a community jobs program. Later, as vice president of the University of Chicago Hospitals, she was assigned the sensitive job of turning people away from the emergency room and finding them more appropriate health care elsewhere. Those clients didn't need emergency care, they simply had no other place to find a doctor.

During Barack's race for the state Senate, Michelle proved to be a fierce campaigner for her husband. On a campaign visit to a tough Chicago neighborhood, Michelle waded into a crowd of thugs who threatened to disrupt the event, ordering them to leave. Ron Carter, publisher of an African-American weekly newspaper in Chicago, saw the incident. He recalled, "There were lots of **radicals** protesting, calling into question [Barack's] loyalty to the community. She came out the back door, and there were a bunch of hoodlum thugs ready to do a full-blast demonstration. She put on her street sense and asked all the guys, 'Y'all got a problem or something?' They all froze, guys who would slap the mayor, who would slap Jesse Jackson in the face, even."

Later, Barack entered his first race for Congress, a Democratic **primary** against U.S. Rep. Bobby Rush, and lost after Rush was able to use his absence on the gun control issue against him.

Barack learned an important lesson from that race. He realized that his desire for the seat was driven solely by his ambition for higher office—that he had simply not made the case to the voters why they should choose him over Rush. Barack knew he would have to wait for an opportunity when he could show that his qualifications were far superior to those of his opponents.

"YES, WE CAN"

That opportunity arrived in early 2004 when he entered the primary for the U.S. Senate. His two opponents were Dan Hynes, the state **comptroller** and son of an influential state

Barack Obama delivers a speech. During his 2004 campaign for the U.S. Senate, he developed his speaking style, learning how to spotlight his command of the issues and inspire, electrify, and touch the emotions of his audiences. He also began to use his now-familiar slogan, "Yes, we can."

senator, Thomas Hynes, and Blair Hull, a millionaire business-man. Because of his father's influence, Hynes had the backing of many of the state's powerful Democratic leaders, while Hull spent enormous amounts of money on an advertising blitz.

But both candidates self-destructed. Shortly before the spring primary, reports of wife abuse surfaced against Hull. As for Hynes, he proved to be a lackluster campaigner who spent little time on the trail, preferring instead to leave his fate in the hands of the state's power brokers.

Barack worked hard that spring, campaigning nonstop. It was during this campaign that Barack's gift for **rhetoric** first surfaced—people were dazzled by his speeches, command of the issues, and an ability to make emotional connections with his audiences.

The campaign also marked the first time Barack used a slogan he would later employ in his coming presidential campaign: "Yes, we can." The slogan meant that voters could send a candidate to Washington to change the way things are done there. While filming a television commercial for the campaign, Barack stepped in front of the camera and said,

❝Now they say we can't change Washington? I'm Barack Obama and I am running for the United States Senate to say, 'Yes, we can.'❞

Voters responded enthusiastically. In the March primary, Barack overwhelmed his rivals: the final percentages were Obama, 53; Hynes, 24; and Hull, 10.

Barack Obama before delivering the keynote speech at the 2004 Democratic National Convention in Boston, July 28, 2004. Barack's speech lit up the convention, suddenly bringing him from the relative obscurity of the Illinois senate to the fore-front of the national political stage.

Preaching Change

Barack's sweeping victory in the 2004 Illinois U.S. Senate primary brought him to the attention of Senator John Kerry of Massachusetts, who had just wrapped up the Democratic nomination for president. Kerry hoped to add some sizzle to that summer's Democratic National Convention in Boston, and so he asked Barack to make the **keynote address**.

THE AUDACITY OF HOPE

Barack's 17-minute speech, titled "The Audacity of Hope," dazzled listeners as he called on a united America to solve the grave problems facing the nation. Speaking before a packed convention hall as well as a national TV audience, Barack said,

Delegates cheer during Barack Obama's keynote address at the 2004 Democratic National Convention. His 17-minute speech made a powerful impression on the audience and was considered a major political event. Barack went on to win his race for the U.S. Senate that fall. And the Obama phenomenon had begun.

❝ There's not a black America and white America and Latino America and Asian America—there's the United States of America. . . . We are one people. ❞

During the speech, it was clear that Barack electrified the crowd. When he mentioned that his mother grew up in Kansas, the Kansas delegation exploded with whoops and whistles. Standing off to the side, Barack's press aide, Julian Green, saw how Barack was able to stoke up the audience. He recalled,

> **"When I looked past the stage and saw how people reacted, when I saw people falling out, people crying, I thought to myself that I had never experienced anything like this, anything this powerful.**
>
> **You know, I'm not sure what this means, but I couldn't help but think, 'Is he the one? Could he really be the one we have been looking for?'"**

STATE OF AMERICAN POLITICS

Barack emerged from the speech as a national political figure whose best days were definitely ahead of him. Kerry did not fare as well—he lost a close election that fall to President George W. Bush. As for Barack, his Republican opponent in the fall Senate race, conservative **pundit** Alan Keyes, was unable to find traction for his campaign as Barack racked up some 70 percent of the vote.

Barack had now won a Senate seat by an overwhelming majority. His keynote address at the 2004 convention was still regarded as one of the major political events of the decade. Shortly after the convention, he wrote a second book based on the message he delivered at the convention. Titled *The Audacity of Hope*, the book spoke about the state of American politics—how it is controlled

African-American Senators

When he won election to the U.S. Senate, Barack became only the fifth African American to take office in the upper house of Congress. Among Barack's predecessors were Hiram Revels, who was appointed to the Senate by the Mississippi legislature in 1870, and Blanche K. Bruce, a former slave who was appointed to the Senate by the Mississippi legislature in 1875.

The first African American elected to the Senate was Edward Brooke of Massachusetts, who took his seat in 1967 and served through 1979. In 1992, Carol Moseley Braun of Illinois became the first African-American woman to win election to the Senate. She remained in the Senate for one term and then served as U.S. ambassador to New Zealand.

by special interests with big money; how the press and pundits often feed on conflict, blowing up mild disagreements into major disputes; and how some political leaders have to compromise their values to get elected. He wrote,

> **" We feel in our gut the lack of honesty, rigor, and common sense in our policy debates, and dislike what appears to be a continuous menu of false or cramped choices. Religious or secular, black, white, or brown, we sense—correctly—that the nation's most significant challenges are being ignored, and that if we don't change course soon, we may be the first generation in a very long time that leaves behind a weaker and more fractured America than the one we inherited. "**

By 2006, *The Audacity of Hope* as well as *Dreams from My Father* were both bestsellers. In that fall's congressional elections,

Barack Obama's Addictions

Barack Obama is addicted to choco-late-peanut protein bars. He also loves Planter's Trail Mix, roasted almonds, pistachios, and raisins. A smoker, he chews Nicorette and Dentyne Ice gums to fight the habit. (When he discussed running for the presidency with Michelle, she consented to the campaign on the condition that he give up cigarettes. Barack agreed, but as the campaign entered the busy primary season in 2008, he returned to smoking.)

One of his favorite meals is his wife's shrimp linguini. His favorite book is *Moby-Dick* by Herman Melville, although he has read all the *Harry Potter* books with his daughters. His love of music is diverse—he listens to folk music by Bob Dylan, jazz by Miles Davis, classical music by Johann Sebastian Bach, and hip-hop by The Fugees. His favorite movies are *Casablanca*, a World War II drama about freedom fighters in North Africa, and *One Flew Over the Cuckoo's Nest*, the story of a man who fights to maintain his identity in a mental institution.

Barack Obama on his way to a Senate vote in 2005. Obama impressed both sides of the political aisle. Richard Lugar, an Indiana Republican senator for 30 years, offered unusually strong praise for Barack: "He does have a sense of idealism and principled leadership, a vision of the future."

Democrats swept into power in the House and Senate. Clearly, the political tide had turned away from the conservatism of the Republican Party, which had controlled both houses of Congress as well as the White House for most of the previous six years. Remembering the lesson he learned in his campaign against Congressman Bobby Rush, Barack knew the time was right to put his credentials against those of others seeking the nation's highest office. In February 2007, Barack announced his intention to seek the presidency in 2008.

IMPRESSIVE VICTORY IN IOWA

From the start, though, his campaign faced tremendous odds. As the front-runner, Senator Hillary Rodham Clinton of New York

Barack Obama at a book signing in Portsmouth, N.H., in 2006. The audio versions of both Barack's books won Grammy Awards for Best Spoken Word Album (*Dreams from My Father* in 2006 and *The Audacity of Hope* in 2008).

had spent years lining up support from Democratic leaders across the country. The senator, a former first lady, was far better known to the electorate than Barack.

Despite campaigning hard throughout the remainder of 2007, Barack found himself unable to make up much ground against Senator Clinton. By the end of the year, things continued to look bleak for the Obama campaign. Polls taken in late December showed Clinton maintaining a 29-point lead over Barack.

The tide soon turned, however. Barack's message of hope, unity, and change was being received enthusiastically among many young people. Barack found a tremendous resource among these supporters, who flocked to volunteer for his campaign. He also made use of the Internet, finding it to be a valuable resource for raising campaign funds.

In the summer of 2007, he started sending teams of young volunteers to Iowa, site of the first **caucuses** of the 2008 primary season. Iowa would be an important first test—whoever won the Iowa caucuses was sure to be regarded as one of the top tier candidates for the nomination. In January 2008, Barack scored an unexpected and impressive victory in Iowa.

BATTLING FOR DELEGATES

Clinton recovered to win the New Hampshire primary less than a week later. She hoped to deliver a knockout punch to Barack in early February by taking most of the 25 so-called Super Tuesday primaries and caucuses, but after the dust settled on Super Tuesday, the two candidates were virtually even. Barack then kicked it into gear, running off a string of eight consecutive primary and caucus wins.

While Barack was compiling an impressive tally of popular votes, far more important in the primary process was his tally of **delegates**, the party officials who would cast their ballots for the nomination that summer at the Democratic National Convention in Denver, Colorado. Under party rules, the number of delegates was allocated to each candidate depending on the vote totals they scored in the contests.

Barack Obama at a campaign stop, early 2007. Obama appealed to many young voters and gained momentum by focusing on the Internet to gather supporters and campaign contributions; using community-organizing skills (for example, opening 31 offices in Iowa); and establishing "Barack Stars" chapters at many high schools.

COMPARED TO KENNEDY

By early January 2008 Barack had staked out the theme for his campaign. It was the same message he first raised in his "Audacity of Hope" speech—that the nation ached for unity and was weary of the partisan bickering that had dominated Washington politics for decades.

That message found favor among two people who are admired among Democratic voters—Massachusetts Senator Ted Kennedy and his niece, Caroline Kennedy, who is the daughter of the late president John F. Kennedy. President Kennedy served from his inauguration in 1961 until his assassination in November 1963.

During his brief presidency, Kennedy inspired millions of Americans with his call for them to take control of their country's destiny. During his inaugural address, Kennedy said,

> **❝ My fellow Americans: ask not what your country can do for you—ask what you can do for your country. ❞**

Caroline Kennedy said she found Barack's call for Americans to unite to be similar to her father's vision. Writing in the *New York Times*, she said,

Barack Obama addresses an audience during a Boston campaign event as Democratic Senator Edward Kennedy looks on, February 4, 2008. Many people have compared Obama to Kennedy's brother, the late president John F. Kennedy, who was also young, energized, vibrant, and inspiring.

" I have never had a president who inspired me the way people tell me that my father inspired them. But for the first time, I believe I have found the man who could be that president—not just for me, but for a new generation of Americans. "

And Senator Kennedy, younger brother of the late president, said,

" Every time I've been asked over the past year who I would support in the Democratic primary, my answer has always been the same. I'll support the candidate who inspires me, inspires us all, who can lift our vision and summon our best hopes. I've found that candidate. "

PARTY NOMINEE

For her part, Clinton seemed unable to separate herself from a long association with old-style Washington politics. Clearly, the nation wanted change. Still, Clinton remained a formidable adversary; among her most dedicated supporters were millions of women who had hoped Clinton would be elected the first female president in the nation's history.

Meanwhile, Barack was also lining up an impressive list of so-called **super delegates**, party officials who would have an important voice at that summer's national convention.

By early June, the long primary season was finally grinding to an end. Clinton had received nearly 18 million popular votes, just a few thousand less than Barack, but Barack's lead in the delegate count finally went over the mark of 2,118—the minimum number needed for the nomination. On the night of June 3, Barack staged a rally in St. Paul, Minnesota to claim the nomination. He said,

" Sixteen months have passed since we first stood together on the steps of the Old State Capitol in Springfield, Illinois. Thousands of miles have been traveled.

Barack Obama at a rally at the Xcel Energy Center in St. Paul, Minnesota, June 3, 2008. With Barack's presidential nomination, Obama mania exploded. Everywhere he went, excited crowds showed wild enthusiasm. Some devoted, and often frenzied, fans would do anything to see or touch the candidate.

Millions of voices have been heard. And because of what you said—because you decided that change must come to Washington; because you believed that this year must be different than all the rest; because you chose to listen not to your doubts or your fears but to your greatest hopes and highest aspirations, tonight we mark the end of one historic journey with the beginning of another—a journey that will bring a new and better day to America. Tonight, I can stand before you and say that I will be the Democratic nominee for president of the United States. "

Barack Obama visits U.S. troops on his 2008 overseas tour. Obama visited Kuwait, Iraq, and Afghanistan to enhance his understanding of U.S. foreign policy and issues related to the Iraq war. He also managed to fit in time to play basketball with some of the military personnel there.

Hitting from Three-Point Range

Throughout the primary campaign, Senator Clinton had questioned Barack's ability to lead the country, pointing out that her youthful adversary had no foreign policy experience. The charge was largely true—during his brief time in the Senate, Barack had few dealings with foreign heads of state or the issues directly related to the wars in Iraq and Afghanistan.

MIDDLE EAST TOUR

Barack knew he had to send a message to voters that he could quickly master foreign policy. And so, a few weeks before the convention, he scheduled a tour of the Iraq and Afghanistan war zones that included meetings with several heads of state in the Middle East.

The press accompanied Barack on the trip, each day sending back stories about the senator's tour. The first stop on the tour was an American military base in Kuwait, a country that borders Iraq. At the base, Barack met with American soldiers and managed to squeeze in time for some basketball. At the end of the game, Barack hit a shot from 30 feet. When Barack nailed the shot, hundreds of soldiers sitting in the bleachers jumped to their feet and cheered. Observing it all, *Washington Post* **columnist** David Broder wrote,

> **What he could not have counted on is the role that luck has played in the events that have surrounded the tour. . . . When, on the first day of the trip, Obama stepped onto a basketball court at the air base in Kuwait and sent his first three-point shot cleanly through the basket, you knew the gods had decided to favor him.**

Renegade and Renaissance

The Obama family members are protected round-the-clock by secret service agents. The Secret Service is an agency of the U.S. Treasury Department that was established to investigate counterfeiting—the printing of phony money. In 1901, the agency's duties were expanded to provide protection to presidents and their families, and in 1968 secret service protection was expanded further to include presidential candidates and their families.

When secret service agents communicate with one another by radio, they refer to the Obama family members by code names. Barack's code name is Renegade while Michelle's is Renaissance. The code names for the children are Radiance for Malia and Rosebud for Sasha.

Barack Obama waves to the crowd as he delivers a speech at the victory column in Berlin, July 24, 2008. Obama's speech riveted thousands of Germans in the audience and inspired listeners all over the world with his message of unity among all races and countries.

SPEECH IN BERLIN

From the Middle East, Barack headed to Europe where he met with the president of France, the chancellor of Germany, and the prime minister of Great Britain. An important moment in the trip occurred in Germany, where Barack delivered a speech before some 200,000 people in the German capital of Berlin, one of the largest gatherings in the city's history.

For many years following the end of World War II, Germany had been a divided country. West Germany grew into a prosperous democracy while East Germany remained under the control of communism and the former Soviet Union. Berlin itself was a

Barack Obama graces the cover of *Esquire* magazine in June 2008. As the campaign continued, Obama was sometimes treated more like a celebrity than a presidential candidate. Some members of the media clamored more for interviews and photos than for Obama's political perspective.

divided city—half under a democratic government with the other half under the rule of the communists. The city was divided by the notorious Berlin Wall, erected in 1961 to keep East Berliners from fleeing to freedom in the western half of the city. But after the collapse of the Soviet Union in 1991, the wall was torn down and the city and country united under a single democratic government.

Speaking to the crowd less than a mile from where the Berlin Wall had divided the city, Barack spoke about the same message of unity he had been preaching on the campaign trail in the United States. He told the crowd that the problems of the world could be solved only by nations working together. He said,

> **❝ The greatest danger of all is to allow new walls to divide us from one another. The walls between old allies on either side of the Atlantic cannot stand. The walls between the countries with the most and those with the least cannot stand. The walls between races and tribes, natives and immigrants, Christian and Muslim and Jew cannot stand. These now are the walls we must tear down. ❞**

WORLD'S BIGGEST CELEBRITY

Barack's speech was heralded as a tremendous success by the Germans and other Europeans in the crowd, who waved American flags as he spoke—a rare sight, inasmuch as President Bush had been unpopular among Europeans, mostly because of his policies on the Iraq war. Back home, the Berlin speech received wide media coverage—pictures of Barack were splashed across major newspapers throughout the United States. Barack's poll numbers soared, as Americans found themselves enthralled by the power of his oratory and his message of change and unity.

Back in the United States, Barack hit the campaign trail again, and his first order of business was to select a running mate—the candidate who would serve as his vice president. Barack was under tremendous pressure from Clinton's supporters to pick the

New York senator as the nominee for vice president, but Barack resisted the pressure and instead selected Senator Joe Biden of Delaware. A senior senator with expertise in foreign affairs and briefly a candidate for the Democratic nomination for president earlier in 2008, Biden proved to be a steady hand and respected advisor to Barack.

Barack officially received the nomination as his party's candidate for president of the United States on August 27 at the 2008 Democratic National Convention in Denver, Colorado. He accepted his nomination the following night in a speech at Invesco Field before a record-setting crowd of 84,000 people.

FINANCIAL CRISIS

In mid-September, the country slipped into a financial crisis as the nation's largest banks found themselves holding too many loans that borrowers could not repay. Large banks teetered on the edge of going out of business—a situation that could lead to a widespread collapse of the nation's economy. During the crisis, Barack urged Congress to quickly adopt a plan to provide $700 billion to the nation's banks to keep them in business. Many people opposed the **bailout** plan, believing that the federal government should have no role in saving failing businesses, but Barack realized the importance of keeping banks open—they provide loans to individuals and businesses that help people buy homes, manufacture goods, and provide jobs to others.

By late September, Barack was again ahead in the polls, aided in large part by his steady performance in the three nationally televised debates against his Republican opponent John McCain.

THE PROMISE OF CHANGE

By election day, few pundits in the country gave McCain much of a chance to win the election. In fact, on November 4, 2008, Barack scored 53 percent of the vote—the first Democrat to win the presidency with more than 50 percent of the popular vote since President Lyndon Baines Johnson won in a landslide in 1964.

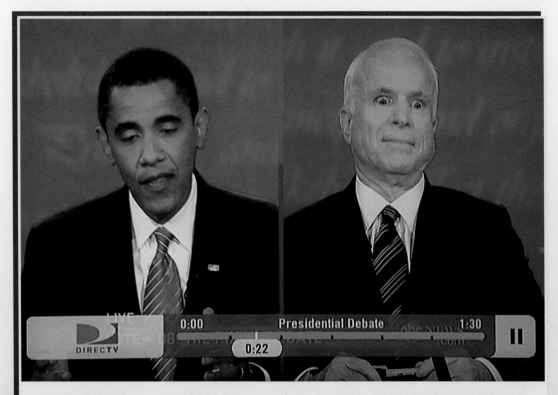

Barack Obama and Republican Senator John McCain during their presidential debate, October 15, 2008. During the campaign, Obama was able to involve many people who had never participated in politics before. He appealed to younger voters and many ethnic groups, while McCain's supporters were mainly conservative white voters.

On election night, the Obama and Biden families celebrated at a rally in Chicago's Grant Park, where more than 240,000 people screamed, cried, jumped up and down, and stood in near disbelief. Millions of people, watching the events unfold on their TVs across America and around the world, felt a renewed sense of hope and optimism.

THE WORK CONTINUES

Soon after claiming victory, Barack went back to work. He continued to use the Internet technologies that served him so well during his campaign. His transition Web site, change.gov, went online just two days after the election, his radio address was videotaped and archived on YouTube for millions of people to view, and a detailed four-page survey was sent via e-mail asking his supporters for their input on how the Obama administration should move forward.

Twenty-four-year-old Chris Hughes, a member of Barack's online operations team, said,

> **What we've learned from this campaign is that there's huge potential for people that haven't been involved in politics. . . . The fundamental premise was to help put the political process into people's own hands. That was the value from the start of the campaign, that was the value at the end of the campaign, and it's not going away.**

REACHING OUT, STEPPING UP

Barack also reached out to friends and adversaries—he named Hillary Clinton secretary of state and also selected Republicans for his cabinet in a sincere desire to unify Washington's bickering factions, living up to the promise of change and unity he had

The White House

In Washington, the Obamas live in the White House at 1600 Pennsylvania Avenue, an address with a long and colorful history. Work on the official residence of the president began in 1792 and was completed in 1800. The first president to live in what was known then as the President's House was John Adams, who spent the last few months of his presidency there.

The White House was burned by the British during the War of 1812, then rebuilt. After World War II, its interior was completely gutted and renovated during the presidency of Harry S. Truman. Later residents gave it a thorough redecoration, most notably the one headed by First Lady Jacqueline Kennedy in the early 1960s. The presidents and their families don't live in the first-floor portion of the building the public sees during tours; rather, their quarters are on the second and third floors.

Barack Obama is being sworn in as the 44th president of the United States as his family looks on, January 20, 2009. The next day Barack was sworn in a second time, because Chief Justice John Roberts administered the oath with one word out of sequence the first time.

pledged so often in his long and ultimately triumphant quest for the presidency.

On January 20, 2009, more than a million people who had traveled distances great and small, gathered in Washington D.C. to witness the historic event—the inauguration of Barack Hussein Obama, a multiracial man of humble beginnings with a distinctly ethnic name and a truly powerful message, as the 44th president of the United States of America.

1961   Barack Hussein Obama Jr. is born on August 4 in Honolulu, Hawaii, to Barack Obama Sr. and Stanley Ann Dunham.

1964   Barack's parents divorce.

1967   Barack moves to Indonesia with his mother following her second marriage to Lelo Soetoro, an Indonesian.

1971   Barack is sent back to Hawaii to live with his maternal grandparents.

1979   Barack graduates from Punahou School in Hawaii and enrolls in Occidental College in California; he later transfers to Columbia University in New York.

1982   Barack Obama Sr. dies in a car accident in Kenya.

1983   Barack graduates from Columbia and takes a job as a financial writer in New York City.

1984   He resigns from his corporate job and takes a job as a community organizer in Chicago.

1988   Barack visits Kenya and enrolls at Harvard Law School.

1989   He meets and starts dating Michelle Robinson, a young attorney who mentors him during a summer job at a Chicago law firm.

1991   He graduates from Harvard and moves back to Chicago to work as a civil rights lawyer.

1992   Barack marries Michelle.

1995   Barack's mother dies of cancer.

1996   Barack wins his first political race, a seat in the Illinois State Senate.

1998   Daughter Malia is born.

2000   Barack loses a primary race for the U.S. House to the incumbent, Bobby Rush.

2001   Daughter Sasha is born.

2004   Barack delivers keynote address at the Democratic National Convention.

   He is elected to the U.S. Senate representing Illinois.

2007   Barack kicks off candidacy for the presidency.

2008   Barack is elected 44th president of the United States.

2009   The Obamas move into the White House.

1979 Plays on a varsity basketball team at Punahou School that wins the Hawaii state championship.

1990 Elected first African-American president of the *Harvard Law Review*.

1992 Heads Illinois Project Vote, which registers 100,000 new voters, mostly in the African-American community.

1995 Publishes *Dreams from My Father*, an autobiography in which he talks about his struggle to understand his racial identity and traces his roots back to Kenya.

2004 Selected by presidential candidate John Kerry to deliver the keynote address at the Democratic National Convention.

2005 Sworn in as only the fifth African-American senator in U.S. history.

2006 Wins Grammy Award for Best Spoken Word Album for the audio book version of *Dreams from My Father*.

Publishes *The Audacity of Hope*, in which he sketches out his plan for national unity and positive change in Washington.

Awarded honorary doctor of laws degree from the University of Massachusetts-Boston.

2008 Wins Grammy Award for Best Spoken Word Album for the audio book version of *The Audacity of Hope*.

Named Person of the Year by *Time* magazine.

bailout—A rescue from financial distress.

caucuses—Events used by some states to award delegates to presidential candidates; in a caucus, voters meet in groups and cast their ballots in public.

civil rights—Rights defined by the U.S. Constitution that guarantee all Americans equal treatment under law, such as the right to vote.

columnist—Newspaper or magazine journalist who offers opinions on politics and other issues of the day.

comptroller—Also known as a controller, an official of the government or a private business responsible for ensuring that money is spent properly.

delegates—Officials of the Republican and Democratic parties selected through primaries and caucuses and designated to cast votes to nominate presidential candidates at the party conventions, based on the number of popular votes the candidates received.

electoral votes—The official votes cast by the Electoral College in the presidential election reflecting the popular votes in the states.

keynote address—A major speech delivered at the opening of national political conventions, or similar events, intended to set the tone and inspire those who attend.

Middle East—Region of southwest Asia and northern Africa marked by turmoil, often prompted by religious differences among its people.

miscegenation—Marriage in which the participants are of different races.

motorcade—Long line of cars, often led and trailed by police vehicles, used to transport a head of state or other dignitary over city streets or highways.

primary—Process used by many states to select nominees for fall elections and award delegates to presidential candidates.

pundit—Writer or broadcaster who offers opinions on political issues in a clever, catchy way.

radical—An agitator who stirs up trouble, often by violent means, to deliver a political message.

rhetoric—Words spoken or written eloquently or effectively, but often insincerely and only for the effect they will have.

scholarship—Financial assistance offered by a school or college to help a student pay the cost of tuition.

super delegates—Delegates to the national political conventions who are not selected by voters; rather, they are party officials, such as governors and members of Congress.

Books and Periodicals

Burton, Tristan. *Indonesia*. New York: Chelsea House, 2006.

Ifill, Gwen. "The Obamas: Portrait of an American Family," *Essence* (September 2008): p. 150.

Merida, Kevin. "The Ghost of a Father," *Washington Post* (December 14, 2007): p. A-12.

Obama, Barack. *The Audacity of Hope: Thoughts on Reclaiming the American Dream*. New York: Three Rivers Press, 2006.

———. *Dreams from My Father: A Story of Race and Inheritance*. New York: Crown, 2004.

Schuman, Michael A. *Barack Obama: We Are One People*. Berkeley Heights, N.J.: Enslow Publishers, 2008.

Truman, Margaret. *The President's House: The Secrets and History of the World's Most Famous Home*. New York: Ballantine, 2005.

Watson, Paul. "As a Child, Obama Crossed a Cultural Divide in Indonesia," *Los Angeles Times* (March 15, 2007): p. A-1.

Web Sites

http://www.barackobama.com
Obama for America, the campaign committee that worked to elect Barack Obama to the presidency, maintains a Web site that explains the issues the 44th president must tackle during his administration.

http://baic.house.gov
Black Americans in Congress is maintained by the Office of the Clerk of the U.S. House of Representatives. The Web site provides students with an extensive history on all African Americans who have served in Congress.

http://www.law.harvard.edu
Harvard Law School maintains a Web site explaining the school's curriculum as well as many issues faced by law students.

http://www.punahou.edu
Punahou School, the private academy in Honolulu, Hawaii, attended by Barack Obama maintains this Web site, outlining the school's activities and providing prospective students with an overview of the school's programs.

ABOUT THE AUTHOR

Hal Marcovitz is a former newspaper reporter who has written more than 100 books for young readers. In 2005, *Nancy Pelosi*, his biography of House Speaker Nancy Pelosi, was named to *Booklist* magazine's list of recommended feminist books for young readers. He lives in Chalfont, Pennsylvania, with his wife Gail and daughter Ashley.